TOP 10 PITCHERS

IN BASEBALL

E **Enslow Publishing**
101 W. 23rd Street
Suite 240
New York, NY 10011
USA
enslow.com

Published in 2016 by Enslow Publishing, LLC
101 W. 23rd Street, Suite 240, New York, NY 10011

Library of Congress Cataloging-in-Publication Data
Aretha, David.
Top 10 pitchers in baseball / David Aretha.
    pages cm. — (Sports greats)
Includes bibliographical references and index.
Summary: "Describes the ten best pitchers in the history of baseball"— Provided by publisher.
Audience: Age: 8-up.
Audience: Grade: 4 to 6.
ISBN 978-0-7660-7408-8 (library binding)
ISBN 978-0-7660-7406-4 (pbk.)
ISBN 978-0-7660-7407-1 (6-pack)
1. Pitchers (Baseball)—Rating of—United States—Juvenile literature. I. Title. II. Title: Top ten pitchers in baseball.
GV871.A74 2016
796.357'22—dc23

                         2015028586

Printed in the United States of America

To Our Readers: We have done our best to make sure all website addresses in this book were active and appropriate when we went to press. However, the author and the publisher have no control over and assume no liability for the material available on those websites or on any websites they may link to. Any comments or suggestions can be sent by e-mail to customerservice@enslow.com.

Photos Credits: Cover, p. 1 Rob Leiter/MLB/Getty Images Sport/Getty Images (Clayton Kershaw); p. 5 Christian Petersen/Getty Images Sport/Getty Images; pp. 7, 8, 20 Mark Rucker/Transcendental Graphics, Getty Images Sport/Getty Images; p. 11 Photo File/MLB Photos/Hulton Archive/Getty Images; p. 12 Bruce Bennett/Getty Images; p. 15 Henry Groskinsky/The LIFE Images Collection/Getty Images; p. 16 Transcendental Graphics/Archive Photos/Getty Images; p. 19 George Strock/The LIFE Picture Collection/Getty Images; pp. 23, 29, 31 Focus On Sport/Getty Images; p. 24 Mark Kauffman/The LIFE Images Collection/Getty Images; pp. 27, 28, 36 Rich Pilling/MLB Photos/Getty Images Sport/Getty Images; p. 32 Stephen Dunn/Getty Images Sport Classic/Getty Images; p. 35 John Iacono/Sports Illustrated/Getty Images; p. 39 Elsa/Getty Images Sport/Getty Images; p. 40 Peter Muhly/AFP/Getty Images; p. 43 Cameron Spencer/Getty Images Sport/Getty Images; p. 44 Jamie Squire/Getty Images Sport/Getty Images.

★ CONTENTS ★

★ Introduction ★

Minor league pitcher Steve Dalkowski may have been the fastest-throwing pitcher ever. Unfortunately, Dalkowski never reached the major leagues because he struggled to throw strikes. In one minor league game in 1957, he struck out 24 batters but walked 18. He once threw six wild pitches in a row. Another time, his pitch ripped a batter's earlobe off. One of his fastballs broke umpire Doug Harvey's mask and knocked him 18 feet backward. In another game, he hit the guy in the on-deck circle!

It helps to throw hard, but to succeed a pitcher must have great control—that is, he must throw the ball exactly where he wants to throw it. Greg Maddux didn't throw very fast, but with his pinpoint accuracy he won 355 games.

A good pitcher will also confuse the batter. He'll throw a variety of pitches—fastball, curveball, slider, changeup, and so on—to keep the hitter guessing. A masterful hurler will fire to all parts of the strike zone: top, bottom, left, right, but rarely down the middle. Pitchers also try to change speeds. A 95-mile-per-hour (mph) fastball followed by an 80-mph changeup—thrown with the same arm motion as the fastball—will fluster the batter.

In the 1800s, pitchers threw mostly fastballs. Over time, their pitches evolved. Candy Cummings reportedly was the first to toss a curveball. In the 1930s, Carl Hubbell perfected the screwball, which breaks in the opposite direction of a curve. (Don't try it; it destroys pitchers' arms!) Ron Guidry relied heavily on a slider in

1978 when he went 25–3 for the New York Yankees. A slider is sort of a hybrid between a fastball and curveball. During Guidry's era, reliever Bruce Sutter mastered the split-fingered fastball. It comes in like a fastball but nose-dives at the last moment.

Today's major league pitchers do it all. Many throw 95 to 100 mph and have a mix of other pitches in their repertoire. The curveball, slider, and changeup are most common, but there are alternates, too. A 12-to-6 curveball drops more vertically than horizontally. A cut fastball

Clayton Kershaw's deception gives him an edge; the batter doesn't see the ball until it's on its way.

(cutter) is like a fastball but it breaks a little at the last instant. Mariano Rivera earned a record 652 saves relying primarily on his cutter.

Clayton Kershaw possesses a great repertoire as well as a couple of handy tricks, including a herky-jerky motion. He also holds the ball close to his body before he throws. Batters thus have a hard time seeing the ball until it's well into flight. Kershaw also succeeds because he throws his pitches for strikes—a skill that poor Steve Dalkowski never quite figured out.

★ CY YOUNG ★

Nickname:	Cyclone
Teams:	Cleveland Spiders, 1890–1898; St. Louis Perfectos, 1899–1900; Boston Americans/Red Sox, 1901–1908; Cleveland Naps, 1909–1911; Boston Rustlers, 1911
Position:	Right-handed starter
Number:	None
Year of Note:	1901; went 33–10, leading AL in wins and ERA (1.62)

When Cy Young debuted in the National League (NL) in 1890, the opposing Chicago Colts players laughed at him. *Sporting Life* magazine noted his "weirdness of appearance." The farm boy stood six feet, two inches—unusually tall for his day—and wore a uniform that was *way* too small and tight. The Colts players snickered at the pitcher…until they stepped into the batter's box.

"The game began and the Chicago batters strode to the plate arrogant and confident," *Sporting Life* reported. But then Young began to fire blazing fastballs. "One after the other they threw down their bats and returned to the bench puzzled and baffled."

Cy Young earned the win that day, one of his 511 career victories. Young is, in fact, the winningest pitcher in Major League Baseball

(MLB) history. The number two guy on the all-time list, Walter Johnson, earned 417 triumphs. No one else has won more than 373.

Born Denton True Young in Gilmore, Ohio, Young built his muscles doing farm chores. He fired the ball so fast that he earned the nickname "Cyclone," which was later shortened to Cy. Besides his fastball, Young fooled hitters with two types of curveballs. "One of them sailed in there as hard as my fastball and broke in reverse," he told sportswriter Francis J. Powers. "It was a narrow curve that broke away from [a right-handed] batter and went in just like a fastball. And the other was a wide break."

Young's career included 511 wins—that's nearly 100 more than all other pitchers throughout baseball's rich history.

When Young played, pitchers frequently threw a lot of innings. In 1884, for example, Old Hoss Radbourn pitched 73 complete games and compiled a record of 59–11. However, these men were not as big and strong as Young, and their arms wore out after a few years. Young pitched twenty-two seasons in the majors, and he compiled records that have never been broken. He owns all-time MLB records for wins, losses (316), games started (815),

In 1908, when Young was forty-one years old, he became the oldest man to ever pitch three no-hitters. This record lasted for eighty-two years.

games finished (749), innings pitched (7,356), and batters faced (29,565).

Young led his league in victories five times, with a high of 36 in 1892. In 1901, the American League's (AL) first year of existence, he won the "pitcher triple crown." That means he paced the league in wins (33–10 record), ERA (1.62), and strikeouts (158).

In 1903, Young helped the Boston Americans win the very first World Series, as he personally beat Pittsburgh twice. A year later, he tossed the first perfect game of the century. In a contest that lasted just eighty-five minutes, Young retired all 27 Philadelphia A's batters. "When the game was finished it looked like all the fans came down on the field and tried to shake my hand," he told Powers. "One gray-haired fellow jumped the fence back of third and shoved a five-dollar bill into my hand."

In 1956, one year after Young died, MLB introduced a trophy in his honor. To this day, the best pitcher in each league is presented the Cy Young Award.

★ CHRISTY MATHEWSON ★

Nickname:	*Matty*
Teams:	*New York Giants, 1900–1916*
Position:	*Right-handed starter*
Number:	*None*
Year of Note:	*1908; set still-standing NL record for wins (37–11) and led league in ERA (1.43) and strikeouts (259)*

As a child in Factoryville, Pennsylvania, Christy Mathewson longed to pitch for the hometown team. He was too young to play with these grown-up ballplayers, so he settled for being the team batboy and mascot. Then one day when Christy was thirteen, the pitcher became ill. The club allowed the eager lad to try out during a warm-up game. Mathewson struck out the first batter and half the hitters he faced. "You'll do, son," said the team captain.

A star was born.

"Mathewson was the greatest pitcher who ever lived," asserted Connie Mack, who managed the Philadelphia Athletics from 1901 to 1950. "He had knowledge, judgment, perfect control, and form. It was wonderful to watch him pitch when he wasn't pitching against you."

"Matty" grew to become a tall, handsome gentleman. He excelled in the classroom and attended Bucknell College, where he starred in baseball and football. Around that time, he learned to throw his famous "fadeway," which broke in the opposite direction of a curveball.

The New York Giants of the National League wisely signed Mathewson in July 1900. They proceeded to let him go after the season and then trade for him in December. When he struggled a little in 1902, Giants manager Horace Fogel wanted to move him to first base. John McGraw, who replaced Fogel as manager that summer, thought that was the dumbest idea he had ever heard.

Christy Mathewson was known for being both strong and composed, whether he was on the pitcher's mound or out in public.

"Trying to make a first baseman out of Mathewson!" McGraw exclaimed. "There's a kid with as fine a pitching motion as I ever saw and as much stuff as any young fellow to come up in years. He'll pitch from now on."

And did he ever! From 1903 to 1905, Mathewson posted records of 30–13, 33–12, and 31–9 while leading the National League in

Mathewson bewildered more than a few batters with the famous pitch he called the "fadeaway," which is now known as a screwball.

strikeouts each year. His 37 victories in 1908 remain a modern (meaning since 1901) NL record. From 1903 to 1914, Mathewson went 327–133 with 2.00 ERA. His 373 career victories set an NL record. Warren Spahn tied the mark, but no one has broken it. Only Cy Young and Walter Johnson have won more major league games.

Throughout his career, Matty was baseball's finest role model. "Christy Mathewson brought something to baseball no one else had ever given the game," wrote sportswriter Grantland Rice. "He handed the game a certain touch of class, an indefinable lift in culture, brains, and personality."

In 1905, Mathewson faced the Athletics three times in the World Series and threw three shutouts. To this day, many consider it the greatest performance in World Series history. When New York fans saw Matty exit the clubhouse after the final game, they hoisted him onto their shoulders. They paraded their hero around the area, singing and shouting his name.

Mathewson seemed to live a charmed life, but then World War I broke out. He was supposed to go to France to captain the U.S. Army's Chemical Warfare Division. But during a training exercise, Matty accidentally inhaled poisonous gas. He was later diagnosed with tuberculosis. The legendary athlete gradually found it hard to read, write, talk, and move his limbs. In 1925, Mathewson died from his illness at age forty-five.

★ WALTER JOHNSON ★

Nickname:	*Big Train*
Teams:	*Washington Senators, 1907–1927*
Position:	*Right-handed starter*
Number:	*None*
Year of Note:	*1913; went 36–7, leading AL in wins, ERA (1.14), and strikeouts (243)*

According to baseball lore, Indians batter Ray Chapman struck out on just two pitches against Washington Senators pitcher Walter Johnson. On an overcast day in Cleveland, Chapman could barely see Johnson's blazing blur of a fastball. After taking two strikes, he left the batter's box and walked toward the dugout. Umpire Billy Evans told Chapman that he still had one strike left. "You can have it," the defeated hitter replied. "It wouldn't do me any good."

They called Walter Johnson the "Big Train" because his teammates rode him to victory. His 417 wins rank second all time behind Cy Young's 511. They are the most victories in "modern" MLB history, meaning since 1901, when the American League began.

Incredibly, Johnson won all of those games with the mediocre Senators, a team that rarely contended for the AL title in his twenty-one years with the club. Johnson's 110 shutouts are a major league record. Often he *had* to throw a shutout for his team to win the game: On twenty-six occasions, he lost 1–0. On July 1, 1920, he defeated Boston 1–0 by throwing a no-hitter. He would have had a perfect game except his second baseman booted a groundball for an error.

The Big Train's repertoire consisted of only one pitch: the fastball. Because he threw with an easy sidearm motion, hitters didn't expect the ball to arrive so fast. But it did. As opposing batter Ping Bodie said, "You can't hit what you can't see." Legendary hitter Ty Cobb provided his own

Walter Johnson's fastball fooled many a batter. He looked so relaxed as he pitched that the hitter didn't expect the incredible speed.

assessment of the Big Train: "Just speed, raw speed, blinding speed, too much speed."

While today's star amateur players sign multimillion-dollar contracts, Johnson's beginnings were much more humble. As

Walter "Big Train" Johnson holds the record for the most shutouts at 110.

an eighteen-year-old in 1906, he joined the Weisner Telephone Company. For $75 a month, he dug post holes and pitched for the company's team. The next year, the Senators acquired him for a $100 signing bonus and $350 a month. (Today's star pitchers earn thousands of dollars for each pitch!)

Johnson peaked during the 1910s. In that decade, he went 265–143 with a 1.59 ERA and led the AL in strikeouts nine times. In 1913, he became the first (and only) pitcher with at least 30 wins and an ERA below 1.15. En route to a 36–7 record that year, he reeled off streaks of 10, 11, and 14 wins. At one point that season, he pitched 56⅔ consecutive innings without allowing a run. That remains an AL record. Johnson led the league in strikeouts 12 times, and his 3,509 whiffs were a major league record until broken by Nolan Ryan in 1983.

Johnson didn't reach the World Series until his eighteenth season, in 1924. Ironically, his only win in that series came as a reliever—in the Game 7 finale. He pitched a shutout from the ninth through twelfth innings as the Senators won their only World Series title in their sixty-year history. In 1936, Johnson was among the first six players inducted into the Baseball Hall of Fame.

Nickname:	None
Teams:	Many Negro League teams; Cleveland Indians, 1948–1949; St. Louis Browns, 1951–1953; Kansas City Athletics, 1965
Position:	Right-handed starter
Number:	Many
Year of Note:	1948; went 6–1 with a 2.48 ERA as a forty-two-year-old rookie with the Cleveland Indians

Because of his skin color, Leroy "Satchel" Paige couldn't pitch in the major leagues. So he pitched everywhere else. He toiled for many Negro League teams—sometimes two of them in two days.

"One day I pitched a no-hitter for the [Pittsburgh] Crawfords against the Homestead Grays [in Washington, D.C.]," he wrote in his book *Maybe I'll Pitch Forever*. "That was on July 4. I remember because somebody kept shooting off firecrackers every time I got another batter out. Those firecrackers still were popping when I ran out of the park, hopped into my car, and drove all night to Chicago. I got there just in time to beat Ted Trent and the Chicago American Giants one to nothing in twelve innings. And that same day, somebody said I was supposed to be pitching in Cleveland."

Paige was one of a kind. He traveled from team to team in his own car, and he sometimes played guitar in Louis Armstrong's orchestra. His words of wisdom are still quoted today. "Age is a case of mind over matter," he said. "If you don't mind, it don't matter." His philosophy on life? "Don't look back," he said. "Something might be gaining on you."

Leroy earned his nickname at age seven, when he was employed to load satchels (suitcases) at an Alabama railroad station. As a troublemaking child, Paige wound up in reform school. When he was released at age seventeen, he began the most amazing career in baseball history.

Throughout his career, to see Satchel Paige pitch was an unforgettable sight, as this high kick demonstrates.

In his notebooks, Paige recorded the results of his games. According to his notes, he pitched in more than 2,500 games for 250 teams and accumulated around 2,000 victories. He also claimed to throw 50 no-hitters, win three games in one day, and strike out 22 batters in one contest. Satchel pitched many "barnstorming" games (informal exhibitions) against major leaguers. Paige "was the best I ever saw,"

Among his repertoire of pitches, Paige had fastballs that he named "Little Tommy" and "Long Tommy."

Hall of Fame hurler Bob Feller once said. "And I'm judging him on the way he overpowered or outwitted some of the best big-league hitters of his day."

Paige fired two fastballs. He nicknamed the blazing one "Little Tommy" and the supersonic one "Long Tommy." He called his curveball a "bee ball" because it would "be where I want it to be."

In 1947, Jackie Robinson famously broke the major league color barrier. "Somehow I always thought it would be me," Paige said. The next year, he did debut in the majors. In 1948, as a forty-two-year-old for the Cleveland Indians, he posted a 6–1 record with a 2.48 ERA. At age forty-five in 1953, he went 12–10 for the St. Louis Browns and made the MLB All-Star Game.

Paige didn't limit his pitching to the United States. He toiled in Cuba, Mexico, and the Dominican Republic. In 1935, Dominican dictator Rafael Trujillo formed a super team, which included Paige and other Negro League stars. Surrounded by armed soldiers as they played, they felt a great deal of pressure to prevail. "You never saw ol' Satch throw harder…," Paige wrote.

In 1965, at age fifty-eight, Satchel returned to the major leagues for one game, pitching three innings for the Kansas City Athletics. Fans shook their heads in amazement as he yielded no runs and just one hit. For Paige, age just didn't seem to matter.

★ SANDY KOUFAX ★

Nickname:	*The Left Arm of God*
Team:	*Brooklyn Dodgers, 1955–1957;*
	Los Angeles Dodgers, 1958–1966
Position:	*Left-handed starter*
Number:	*32*
Year of Note:	*1965; won NL pitcher triple crown, set MLB record with 382 strikeouts, and won World Series MVP Award*

For four glorious seasons (1963–1966), Sandy Koufax dominated like no other pitcher ever. Hitters couldn't touch his fastball. "He throws a 'radio ball,'" said opposing batter Gene Mauch, "a pitch you hear but you don't see." His sharp-breaking curveball also frustrated hitters. "Trying to hit him," remarked slugger Willie Stargell, "was like trying to drink coffee with a fork."

Koufax was so amazing that it's hard to believe he started pitching almost by accident—and that at age thirty he left the game for good.

The unusual story of Sandy Koufax began in Brooklyn, New York. From a Jewish family, Koufax lived in the same neighborhood as Buddy Hackett (future comedian) and Larry King (future talk show host). He played on the baseball team at Lafayette High

School but didn't pitch—nor did he hit very well as the team's first baseman. Basketball was Sandy's game, and he earned a basketball scholarship to the University of Cincinnati.

When Koufax learned that U of C's baseball squad was going on a spring trip to New Orleans, he joined that team, too. The hard-throwing left-hander excelled on the mound for the Bearcats, fanning 51 batters in 32 innings as a freshman. In December 1954, before his nineteenth birthday, he signed with the NL's Brooklyn Dodgers.

Koufax pitched for the Dodgers in 1955 and even threw a two-hit shutout. But again, baseball did not define his life. That fall, Brooklyn won its first World Series, defeating the rival New York Yankees. While teammates indulged in wild celebration, Koufax spent the evening attending an architecture class at Columbia University.

For six seasons, Koufax struggled with his control. After posting an 8–13 record in 1960, he considered retiring from baseball to sell light fixtures. He also asked the Dodgers to trade him. "We stayed with you this

Once he mastered control of the ball, Sandy Koufax became notorious for his blisteringly fast left-handed pitches.

Between 1962 and 1965, Koufax triumphed with an annual no-hitter, and in 1965 he threw a perfect game against the Cubs.

long," general manager Buzzy Bavasi replied, "we might as well keep you."

In 1961, Koufax began to blossom. He started to exercise more. He altered the grip on his curveball. And he changed his pitching motion, which improved his control. In 1961, he went 18–13, led the league with 269 strikeouts, and made the NL All-Star team. The next season, he finished 14–7 with a league-best 2.54 ERA. Then the real fun began.

In 1963, Koufax won the pitcher triple crown, meaning he led the league in wins (25–5), ERA (1.88), and strikeouts (306). He also captured the Cy Young Award, NL MVP Award, and World Series MVP Award (2–0, 1.50 ERA). In 1964, he finished 19–5 with another ERA crown (1.74).

From 1962 through 1965, Koufax threw a no-hitter every year, including a perfect game in 1965 against the Chicago Cubs. In 1965 and 1966, he captured two more triple crowns and Cy Young Awards. He went 26–8, 2.04 in 1965 while setting a major league record with 382 strikeouts. Again he led the Dodgers to the championship, going 2–1, 0.38 in the World Series.

Koufax went 27–9, 1.73 in 1966, but he couldn't pitch anymore. His left elbow throbbed in pain and couldn't be fixed. "In those days, there was no surgery," he said years later. In 1972, at age thirty-six, Koufax became the youngest man ever inducted into the Baseball Hall of Fame.

★ NOLAN RYAN ★

Nickname:	Ryan Express
Teams:	New York Mets, 1966, 1968–1971;
	California Angels, 1972–1979;
	Houston Astros, 1980–1988;
	Texas Rangers, 1989–1993
Position:	Right-handed starter
Numbers:	30, 34
Year of Note:	1973; set MLB record with 383 strikeouts (still stands)

It was July 15, 1973, and the "Ryan Express" was rolling. At Tiger Stadium in Detroit, Nolan Ryan had a no-hitter going with two outs in the ninth inning. He had struck out 17 batters, and Tigers hitter Norm Cash had fanned three times. Now Cash strode to the plate with a table leg!

Umpire Ron Luciano told the Tigers slugger that he couldn't bat with a table leg. "Why not?" Cash retorted. "I won't hit him anyway." The hopeless hitter tossed the wood aside and grabbed a real bat. He then popped out to conclude the no-hitter.

Nolan Ryan was the most "unhittable" pitcher in baseball history. He fired a fastball in excess of 100 mph, and his curveball was nasty, too. Ryan allowed just 6.56 hits per nine innings during his career, the lowest number among hurlers with at least 1,000 innings pitched. In 1983, he broke Walter Johnson's major league record of 3,508 strikeouts. He then became the first man to fan 4,000 batters…and then 5,000!

The legend of Nolan Ryan began in the small town of Alvin, Texas. Young Nolan lived a simple life. He fished, climbed trees, swung from ropes, and liked to throw things. As a pitcher for Alvin High School, where he was voted "Most Handsome," Ryan struck out almost everybody. In one seven-inning game, he fanned 21! Nolan broke bones in catchers' hands, and many batters refused to face him.

Nolan Ryan's fastball often topped 100 mph, and he had a nerve-racking curveball, too.

At the age of thirty-three, Ryan signed with the Houston Astros. He pitched his last no-hitter at the age of forty-three.

In 1963, New York Mets scout Red Murff came to watch him. He reported that the "skinny" right-hander "has the best arm I've seen in my life."

Ryan debuted with the Mets in 1969, but he had trouble throwing his fastball for strikes. After five seasons, he was 29–38 and had walked too many batters. After being traded to the California Angels in December 1971, he almost quit. "I would have gotten a job as a laborer, and that would have been it," he said. But then he got better. In 1973, he won 21 games with 383 strikeouts, setting a major league record that still stands. The next year, he earned a career-high 22 wins while whiffing 367.

In 1980, Ryan became MLB's first $1 million-a-year player when he signed with the Houston Astros. The next year, he led the NL with a 1.69 ERA. The "Express" was thirty-four at the time—the age when most pitchers enter a serious decline. Yet he kept rolling along. From ages forty to forty-three, with Houston and then the Texas Rangers, he led his league in strikeouts every year.

Ryan exercised religiously, but so did other pitchers. Somehow, he continued to defy age. In 1990, he threw a no-hitter at age forty-three. On May 11, 1991, he told his pitching coach, "I don't know how you feel at 44, but I feel old today. My back hurts. My ankle hurts." Then he started the game and threw his seventh career no-hitter. That's three more than any other pitcher.

In 1993, Ryan concluded his twenty-seventh MLB season (also a record). He had amassed 324 wins and 5,714 strikeouts—839 more than anyone else.

★ GREG MADDUX ★

Nickname:	*The Professor*
Team:	*Chicago Cubs, 1986–1992, 2004–2006; Atlanta Braves, 1993–2003; Los Angeles Dodgers, 2006, 2008; San Diego Padres, 2007–2008*
Position:	*Right-handed starter*
Numbers:	*31, 36, 30*
Year of Note:	*1995; led NL in wins (19–2) and ERA (1.63) to win his fourth straight Cy Young Award*

Greg Maddux could throw a baseball *exactly* where he wanted to. Case in point: In 2008, Maddux was fooling around in the bullpen at Chicago's Wrigley Field. He announced that he was going to throw the ball off a chair, have it bounce off the wall, and then cross the plate. San Diego general manger Kevin Towers witnessed the amazing feat. He told reporter Tim Kurkjian, "The second time he tried it, he hit the leg of a metal chair, the ball bounced off the wall, and ricocheted right over the plate."

All his life, Maddux performed amazing feats with a baseball. He stood only six feet tall—short for a pitcher—and didn't throw very hard. Yet with incredible control, and by consistently outsmarting hitters, he won 355 games. That's eighth all-time. No pitcher whose career began after World War II has won that many games. Moreover, no pitcher was ever more reliable. Maddux is the only pitcher ever to win at least 15 games 17 years in a row. As for control, he led the NL in fewest walks per inning nine times.

As a kid in Las Vegas, Nevada, Greg benefited by playing with his older brother, Mike Maddux, a future major league pitcher. Moreover, both boys trained with a pitching expert named Ralph Medar. In his Baseball Hall of Fame induction speech Greg Maddux recalled, "He taught me my basic pitching fundamentals: movement, location, the ability to change speeds, and velocity—in that order."

Greg Maddux wasn't known for throwing hard, but he was an incredibly precise pitcher who could pinpoint exactly where he wanted to throw the ball.

Maddux won the Cy Young Award for 1992–1995. He also won eighteen Golden Glove Awards during his career, a baseball record.

According to Medar, a hard fastball was not as important as throwing pitches on the edges of the strike zone. That's what Maddux did in high school, yet the major college baseball programs didn't offer him a scholarship. They just saw a small pitcher who couldn't throw all that hard. So, Maddux skipped college and entered the MLB Draft after high school. The Chicago Cubs drafted him in the second round.

Just two years later, in 1986, Maddux suited up for the Cubs. At age twenty, he was the youngest pitcher in the major leagues. Cubs manager Jim Frey, Maddux said in his Hall of Fame speech, "thought I was the batboy." Two years later, Maddux made the NL All-Star team. In 1992, he led the league with 20 wins and won the Cy Young Award. For the Atlanta Braves in 1993, 1994, and 1995, he earned the Cy Young every year, giving him four in a row.

Maddux was almost unhittable during this period. In 1994, he led the league with a 1.56 ERA—while the runner-up finished at 2.74. In 1995, Maddux went 19–2 with a 1.63 ERA.

Pitcher John Smoltz marveled at how Maddux out-thought hitters. "Every pitch has a purpose," Smoltz told *Sports Illustrated*. "Sometimes he knows what he's going to throw two pitches ahead. I swear, he makes it look like guys are swinging foam bats against him."

Throughout his career, Maddux helped himself with his defense. He won eighteen Gold Glove Awards, more than any player in history. But he'll always be remembered for his amazing control. "He's the greatest pitcher I've ever seen," Braves pitching coach Leo Mazzone told Kurkjian. "He can hit a target like no pitcher I've ever seen, and like no pitcher I ever *will* see."

★ RANDY JOHNSON ★

Nickname: Big Unit

Team: Montreal Expos, 1988–1989; Seattle Mariners, 1989–1998; Houston Astros, 1998; Arizona Diamondbacks, 1999–2004, 2007–2008; New York Yankees, 2005–06; San Francisco Giants, 2009

Position: Left-handed starter

Numbers: 57, 51, 34, 41

Year of Note: 2001; struck out 372 batters and won the World Series MVP Award

When Randy Johnson pitched, you felt sorry. Sorry for his catcher's hand. Sorry for the left-handed hitters he faced. Sorry for the bird. Sorry for the garage door.

Randy grew up in California—and grew and grew and grew. He eventually would grow to become six-foot-ten and thus became the tallest player in major league history. As a kid, the huge left-hander practiced his blazing fastball by throwing it against the garage door. He fired so hard that the nails in the wood siding would inevitably loosen. His father, Bud, a police officer, would hand him a hammer. "Pound them back in, son," he would say.

Fast forward to a spring training game in 2001. As a dove was enjoying the lovely weather, it swooshed across the infield of an Arizona Diamondbacks-San Francisco Giants game. Unfortunately, the poor thing flew into the path of a Randy Johnson fastball. Poof! Feathers exploded everywhere, and the bird fell to the grass, dead.

Catchers who caught Johnson understood how the bird felt, as the "Big Unit" threw as hard as 102 mph. Early in his major league career, he was inconsistent. For the Seattle Mariners on June 2, 1990, he fired a no-hitter against Detroit. But in 1990, 1991, and 1992, he led the American League in walks. The death of his father, on Christmas Day in 1992, was a turning point.

"From that day on I got a lot more strength and determination to be the best player I could be . . .," Johnson said, "and not to look at things [in games] as pressure, but challenges. What my dad went through was pressure. That was life and death. This is a game."

In 1993, Johnson improved his control dramatically. His fastball/slider combination was often unhittable, especially because he was so tall: The ball came down at hitters at a steep angle. Johnson went 19–8 with 308 strikeouts that year. In 1995, he posted an 18–2

The lanky Randy Johnson could throw pitches that flew across the plate at speeds as high as 102 mph.

Johnson's left-handed pitches came in at such a tight angle that many lefty batters didn't stand a chance against him.

record, led the league in ERA (2.48), and won his first Cy Young Award. He went 20–4 in 1997.

From 1999 to 2002 with Arizona, Johnson won the NL Cy Young Award every year. He went 81–27 over those four seasons and led the NL in ERA three times. He topped the league in strikeouts each year and with astounding totals: 364, 347, 372 (third most since 1886), and 334. On May 8, 2001, he struck out 20 Cincinnati Reds batters. In the 2001 World Series, he went 3–0 with a 1.04 ERA to earn series MVP honors. On May 18, 2004, he fired a perfect game against Atlanta.

Throughout his career, Johnson devastated left-handed hitters. Such batters usually struggle against a lefty pitcher because the ball comes in at a tight angle. In Johnson's career, lefties batted .199 off him with 25 home runs and 598 strikeouts. In games he pitched, many left-handed sluggers simply took the day off.

When he finally retired at age forty-six, Johnson had won 303 games and lost just 166. His 4,875 strikeouts rank second in history, and in 2015 he was inducted into the Baseball Hall of Fame.

★ MARIANO RIVERA ★

Nickname: **Mo**

Team: **New York Yankees, 1995–2013**

Position: **Right-handed closer**

Number: **42**

Year of Note: **2004; recorded a career-high 53 saves**

Poor Ryan Klesko. In the 1999 World Series, the Atlanta Braves' left-handed hitter didn't stand a chance against closer Mariano Rivera. On one pitch, Klesko cracked his bat on a Rivera cut fastball, also known as a cutter. The pitch looked like a fastball, but at the last instant it broke several inches to the left. Klesko got a new bat, but on the next pitch he broke it on a foul ball—with the barrel of the bat flying over the first baseman's head. Rivera's famous pitch was almost literally sawing the bats in half. Later during the plate appearance, Klesko broke a *third* bat while hitting a weak pop-up. Braves teammate Chipper Jones giggled as Klesko walked back to the dugout in defeat.

Rivera also threw a fastball, but he achieved greatness with the cutter. "When he throws it, you think it's straight," lefty hitter Tony Womack told *New York Magazine*, "and the next thing you know, it's on your thumbs." In his nineteen-year career with the New York Yankees, "Mo" rode the cutter to 652 regular-season saves, a major league record. His career 2.21 ERA is the lowest of any pitcher born after the 1800s (minimum 1,000 innings pitched). He is, without doubt, the greatest relief pitcher of all-time.

"When Rivera takes the mound, the other team is sitting in the dugout thinking, 'We've got no chance. It's over,'" Hall of Fame reliever Goose Gossage told *New York Magazine*. "This guy walks into the game, and they are done."

Mariano grew up poor in the Central American country of Panama. He played soccer and baseball for fun, but as a teenager he toiled for three years as a fisherman. "It wasn't an easy job," he told the *New York Daily News*. "It was hard…. Fishing at night. Rain. Day, night. You have to be wise and smart. And quick. You can't fall asleep on those [boats] because you will get in an accident."

With the discipline he learned from fishing—as well as from his strict father—Rivera became

One of Mariano Rivera's signature pitches was a cutter, which fools the batter because it looks like it's coming in straight.

Rivera had such a reputation that when some players saw him take the mound they gave up all hope.

a focused and unrattled pitcher. In his first season in the minor leagues (1990), he allowed just one earned run in 52 innings (0.17 ERA). The Yankees unwisely converted the reliever to a starter, and as a rookie in 1995 he posted a 5.51 ERA. Back to the bullpen he went, and the brilliance began. From 1997 to 2013, he recorded 40 saves in a season nine times, twice hitting 50.

Incredibly, Rivera shined even brighter in October. In 96 postseason games, he went 8–1 with a 0.70 ERA and 42 saves— 24 more than anyone else. It didn't matter if 50,000 fans were screaming and shaking in their shoes. Mo remained calm and effective, helping the Yankees to five World Series titles. As teammate Derek Jeter told the press, "He's the most mentally tough person I've ever played with."

Major League Baseball honored Rivera at the 2013 All-Star Game. When he took the mound in the eighth inning, all other players remained in the dugout. Dramatically, he remained the only person on the field, as players and fans showered him with applause.

★ CLAYTON KERSHAW ★

Nickname:	*The Claw*
Team:	*Los Angeles Dodgers*
Position:	*Right-handed starter*
Number:	*22*
Year of Note:	*2014; led the league in wins (21–3) and ERA (1.77) to win the NL Cy Young Award and MVP Award*

Nobody's perfect in baseball. But sometimes Clayton Kershaw comes close.

Except one game actually *was* perfect!

In 2006, Kershaw and Highland Park High School in Texas battled Justin Northwest in a state play-off game. Through five innings, Clayton had struck out all 15 batters he had faced. Because Highland Park led by 10 runs through five innings, the "mercy rule" was enforced, meaning the game was over. Kershaw had thus pitched an all-strikeout perfect game!

Kershaw finished that year at a perfect 13–0 and was named Gatorade National Baseball Player of the Year. Speaking of Gatorade, flash forward to June 18, 2014, when Kershaw again flirted with perfection. Pitching for the Los Angeles Dodgers, the left-hander authored a no-hitter against the Colorado Rockies. He walked no one and struck out 15. If his shortstop hadn't committed an error, it would have been an ultra-rare perfect game. Afterward, his teammates doused him with Gatorade.

"He's dominating," teammate Matt Kemp told the press that summer. "I'm glad I don't have to face him. He's making some hitters look like they don't have a clue of what they're doing up there. He's got some nasty stuff."

From 2011 through 2014, Kershaw reigned as baseball's best pitcher. He led the NL in ERA all four seasons, with marks of 2.28, 2.53, 1.83, and 1.87. He went 21–5 in 2011 and 21–3 in 2014. He captured the NL Cy Young Award in three of those seasons and finished runner-up in 2012. In 2014, he became first NL pitcher in forty-six years to win the league's MVP Award.

Entering 2015, Kershaw owned a career ERA of 2.48. That was the lowest since the 1910s among pitchers with at least 100 starts and 1,000 innings pitched.

How does he do it? With a quirky delivery and a dazzling

Clayton Kershaw once struck out every batter he faced in a high school game—and he still dominates in the majors.

Kershaw displays a wide range of pitches and a style that is definitely all his own.

repertoire of pitches. During his delivery, Kershaw raises his right leg, lowers it, seems to stop, and then fires. It distracts the hitter. He also holds the ball close to his body before throwing it. "He hides the ball well and it gets on you pretty quick, so it makes him very effective," said Houston Astros shortstop Clint Barmes.

Kershaw's fastball averages about 94 mph, with good movement. Moreover, hitters rarely get good wood on his slider and hard curveball. Both start out looking like a fastball and then break sharply. He once threw a *slow* curveball that broadcaster Vin Scully called "maybe the greatest single pitch I've ever seen." The pitch traveled toward the head of lefty hitter Sean Casey, then landed on the inside corner at the knees for strike three. "Ohhhhh, what a curveball!" Scully exclaimed over the airwaves. "Holy mackerel!... Look at this thing: It's up there, it's right there, and Casey is history."

Despite his success, Kershaw remains kind, humble, and respectful. Clayton and his wife, Ellen, contribute a great deal of time and money to various charities. In 2013, they opened an orphanage in the African country of Zambia. In short, he's a perfect role model for kids ... and sometimes a perfect pitcher.

★ GLOSSARY ★

changeup—A pitch that's thrown with the same arm motion as a fastball but isn't as fast; the speed change is meant to fool the hitter.

color barrier—Refers to the fact that until 1947, African Americans were not permitted to play in the major leagues.

curveball—A pitch thrown with spin, causing the ball to drop vertically and horizontally as it nears home plate.

ERA—Short for "earned run average"; the formula is earned runs allowed divided by innings pitched, times nine.

fan—Strike out.

fireball—Fastball.

Gold Glove—Award bestowed annually by Rawlings to the best defensive player at each position in each league, American and National.

hurler—An informal name for the pitcher.

lore—A specific collection of information, especially historical.

MLB Draft—An annual event in which major league teams select the best eligible amateur players in the United States, Canada, and U.S. territories.

Negro Leagues—Professional leagues for African Americans; played during an era when African Americans were not allowed to play in the major leagues.

perfect game—When a pitcher pitches an entire game and gets every batter out.

repertoire—A pitcher's assortment of pitches; for example, fastball, slider, curveball, and changeup.

shutout—When a pitcher pitches a complete game and does not allow a run.

slider—A breaking ball that is faster than a curveball but doesn't break quite as much.

whiff—An informal term meaning to strike out (verb); strikeout (noun).

wild pitch—A pitch that the catcher can't reach and that allows the baserunner(s) to move up a base.

★ Further Reading ★

Books

Fishman, Jon M. *Clayton Kershaw*. Minneapolis, MN: Lerner, 2014.

Fishman, Jon M. *Mariano Rivera*. Minneapolis, MN: Lerner, 2014.

Graves, Will. *The Best MLB Pitchers of All Time*. Edina, MN: ABDO Publishing, 2014.

Hoblin, Paul. *Great Pitchers of the Negro Leagues*. Edina, MN, ABDO Publishing, 2013.

Lace, William W. *Nolan Ryan: Hall of Fame Baseball Superstar*. New York, NY: Enslow Publishers, 2014.

Websites

Baseball-Reference.com
http://www.baseball-reference.com
Includes endless statistics on every player in major league history.

MLB.com/Kids
http://mlb.mlb.com/mlb/kids
Leads you to the kid sites of all thirty major league teams.

National Baseball Hall of Fame
http://baseballhall.org
Includes profiles on every member of the Hall of Fame, including videos of many.

★ INDEX ★